HELPING YOURSELF HELPING OTHERS

Dealing with

OPIOID MISUSE

Derek Miller

Cavendish Square

New York

Published in 2020 by Cavendish Square Publishing, LLC
243 5th Avenue, Suite 136, New York, NY 10016

Library of Congress Cataloging-in-Publication Data

Names: Miller, Derek L., author.
Title: Dealing with opioid misuse / Derek Miller.
Description: First edition. | New York : Cavendish Square, 2020. | Series: Helping yourself, helping others | Includes bibliographical references and index. Identifiers: LCCN 2018056810 (print) | LCCN 2018057705 (ebook) | ISBN 9781502646286 (ebook) | ISBN 9781502646279 (library bound) | ISBN 9781502646262 (pbk.) Subjects: LCSH: Opioid abuse--Juvenile literature. | Opioid abuse--Treatment--Juvenile literature. | Drug abuse--Juvenile literature.
Classification: LCC RC568.O45 (ebook) | LCC RC568.O45 M55 2020 (print) | DDC 362.29/3--dc23
LC record available at https://lccn.loc.gov/2018056810

Editorial Director: David McNamara
Editor: Caitlyn Miller
Copy Editor: Rebecca Rohan
Associate Art Director: Alan Sliwinski
Designer: Ginny Kemmerer
Production Coordinator: Karol Szymczuk
Photo Research: J8 Media

CONTENTS

TAKE 1-2 TABLE
4-6 HOURS BY
NEEDED FOR PA

OXYCODONE/APA

Generic for:

No Refill

Chapter 1

The Truth About Opioids

I f you or someone you know is struggling with opioid addiction, the situation can seem hopeless. Most people who try to quit start using opioids again. The road to recovery is long, and often opioid misuse gets worse before it gets better. Just because the situation seems hopeless doesn't mean it is. In the end, most people do quit using opioids.

You should keep trying to get help for yourself or someone you know who is misusing opioids. There are effective treatment options. Even if someone

Opposite: Opioids are a class of drugs that include prescription pills like oxycodone and street drugs like heroin.

has tried and failed to quit in the past, they can still succeed in the future. Never give up on yourself—or someone else—who is suffering from addiction.

THE OPIOID CRISIS

Opioids are a broad class of drugs. They include both illegal drugs, like heroin, as well as commonly prescribed medicines, like Vicodin. All opioids work in roughly the same way in the brain, although their strength differs.

Opioids are commonly prescribed for their analgesic effect. Analgesics relieve pain, and opioids are some of the most effective painkillers. Unfortunately, they are also among the most commonly misused drugs. In addition to relieving pain, opioids can cause euphoria in high doses. Euphoria is a feeling of well-being and happiness.

Opioids also cause dependence. This means that the body adapts to the presence of opioids after they are taken repeatedly. When someone who is dependent on opioids stops taking them, it causes withdrawal symptoms that are unpleasant. (Addiction is different from dependence. It is the psychological state of seeking drugs to get high, even in the face of severe consequences.)

Currently, the United States and Canada are in the midst of an opioid crisis. Beginning in the 1990s, doctors began prescribing opioids more and more frequently. Pharmaceutical companies assured

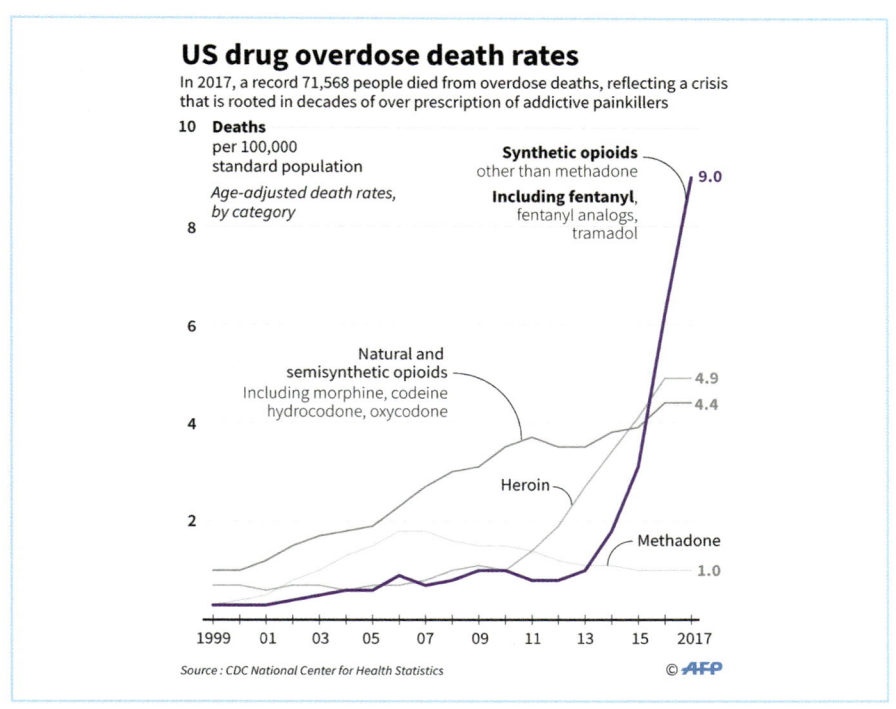

US drug overdose death rates

In 2017, a record 71,568 people died from overdose deaths, reflecting a crisis that is rooted in decades of over prescription of addictive painkillers

Source : CDC National Center for Health Statistics © AFP

This graph shows the number of deaths from opioid overdoses per 100,000 deaths between the years 1999 and 2017.

doctors that the new opioids they created were not addictive. This turned out not to be the case. More and more pain patients unknowingly became dependent on opioids.

As more and more opioids were prescribed, some were diverted to the black market. This fueled the market for illegal opioids. Heroin smuggling increased to take advantage of the new demand. When the health-care industry realized that opioid dependence was on the rise due to overprescribing, many people dependent on opioids saw their prescriptions disappear. Some turned to illegal opioids to stave off withdrawal.

The result of these circumstances is the current opioid crisis. Between 1999 and 2016, the rate of fatal drug overdoses in the United States tripled. About two-thirds of fatal drug overdoses are due to opioids. This means more people die from opioids than every other drug combined. The deadliness of opioids results from the large number of people who misuse them as well as their high risk of overdose.

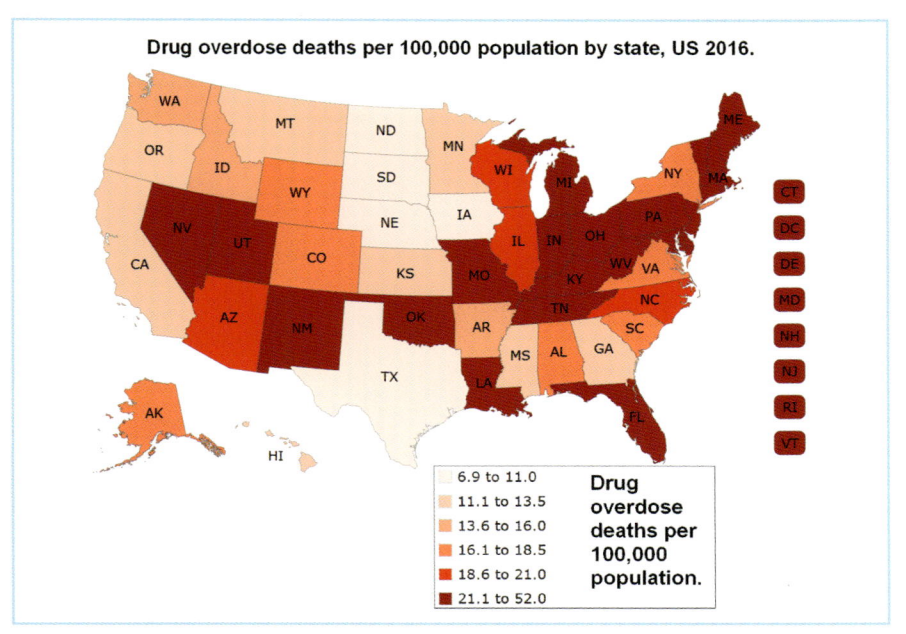

Drug overdose deaths per 100,000 population by state, US 2016.

Legend:
- 6.9 to 11.0
- 11.1 to 13.5
- 13.6 to 16.0
- 16.1 to 18.5
- 18.6 to 21.0
- 21.1 to 52.0

Drug overdose deaths per 100,000 population.

Drug addiction and resulting overdoses hit certain regions of the country harder than others.

When opioids are used as prescribed by a doctor, overdoses are rare. There is a significant margin of error for how much a person can take for pain relief versus how much will kill them. Unfortunately, that difference is much narrower when opioids are taken recreationally. The amount needed to get high is quite close to the fatal amount. In 2017, on average, 115 Americans died every day from an opioid overdose.

THE BASICS OF OPIOIDS

Opioids affect opioid receptors in the brain. These receptors work with naturally occurring compounds in the brain, such as endorphins. Endorphins help the body mask pain and cause feelings like the "runner's high." When opioids are taken, they work on these same opioid receptors, but opioids are taken in much higher amounts than naturally occurring endorphins.

The term "opioid" refers to many different drugs. It comes from the word "opium." Opium is

the dried latex collected from the seedpod of an opium poppy. While related to the poppies that grow in gardens around the world, opium poppies are a

This opium poppy has been scored, and the latex (the white liquid) inside is visible.

specific species of the flower. Opium has been used for thousands of years for its painkilling effects. It is illegal in most countries today because it contains opioids.

In the early 1800s, morphine was isolated from opium. Later, so was codeine. These two compounds are now prescription opioids. Sometimes, you may see the word "opiate" used instead of "opioid." Opiates are derived from opium. They include morphine, codeine, and heroin, which is created from morphine. Technically, opioids that were created in a lab are not opiates. But all opiates are opioids. Often, the two terms are used interchangeably. Today, "opioid" is usually preferred since it refers to the whole class of related drugs, regardless of how they are made.

In the 1900s, many new opioids were synthesized in labs. These drugs are now prescription opioids in countries around the world. Two of the most common opioids in the United States are hydrocodone and oxycodone. Hydrocodone is often called by its brand name: Vicodin. Oxycodone is an ingredient in two common brand-name medications: Percocet and OxyContin. Percocet is a mix of oxycodone and acetaminophen (the active ingredient in Tylenol). OxyContin is extended-release oxycodone—the extended release means pain patients do not have to take it as frequently. Numerous other opioids are prescribed—and misused—such as hydromorphone (Dilaudid), oxymorphone, and methadone.

Heroin is not prescribed in the United States, although it is in some other countries. However, heroin is smuggled into the country and sold on the street illegally. The fact that it is distributed this way makes it even more dangerous than prescription opioids. Unlike prescriptions, the exact strength of heroin is not known to the user. Street heroin is only about 40 percent pure heroin on average, but the exact amount varies because it is "cut" with other substances. This means the same amount of street heroin that was not fatal to a user one day may result in an overdose the next.

In 2014, drug cartels began mixing fentanyl with the heroin they sold. Fentanyl is an opioid that is about 50 times stronger than heroin. It is also prescribed in cases of extremely hard-to-treat pain, usually for cancer patients. When sold as a street drug, fentanyl's potency makes it very dangerous. If drug dealers fail to cut it properly by diluting the fentanyl with other powders, users will overdose and die. There is no room for error. Some drug dealers sell fentanyl as counterfeit heroin or counterfeit prescription drugs. Fake pills are made to look like Vicodin, Percocet, or OxyContin. Instead, these pills contain an unknown quantity of the extremely powerful fentanyl.

Fentanyl is partially responsible for the recent surge in opioid overdoses. Before 2013, only 15 percent of fatal opioid overdoses involved fentanyl. By 2016, 46 percent did, and that number continues to climb. Most people who overdose on fentanyl believed they were buying heroin or prescription pills instead.

Seventeen-year-old Cole Nicholls from Ottawa spoke about the dangers of fake pharmaceuticals to the *Ottawa Citizen* in 2017. He recounted how he had left home at the age of fourteen to live on the street and chase the high of opioids. Over the years, he lost numerous friends to a local drug known as "Percs." It was, in fact, fentanyl made to look like Percocet. Despite the public stigma of drug use, Nicholls gave an on-the-record interview to protect

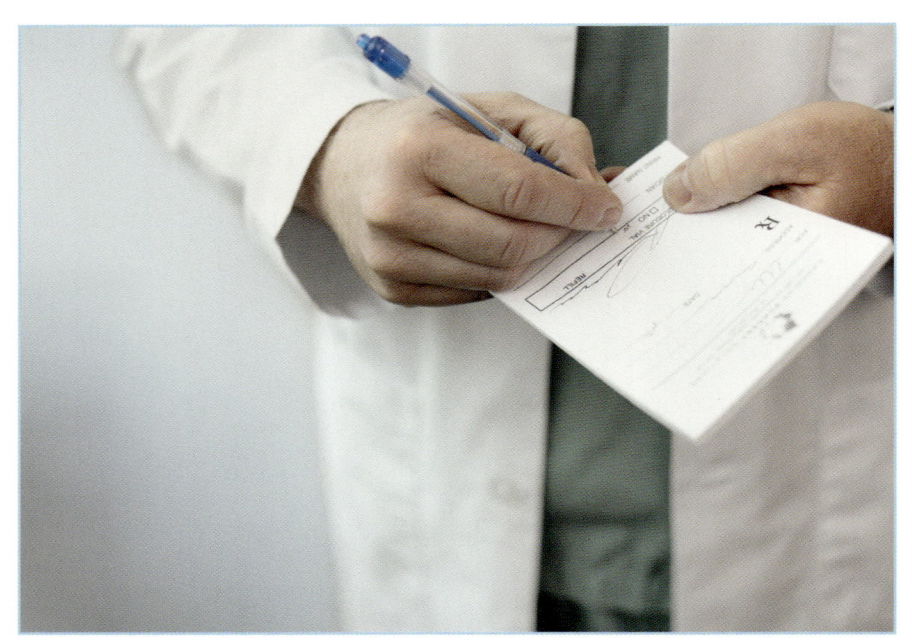

Many people who develop a problem with opioids first misuse opioids that were prescribed by a doctor.

teens from the danger of Percs. He wanted to warn others not to begin taking opioids. In the interview, Nicholls talked about his two previous overdoses and how his friends performed CPR to save him. In 2018, Nicholls overdosed and died after relapsing at the age of eighteen.

THE MANY FACES OF OPIOID ADDICTION

Opioid addiction is a disease that affects people of all backgrounds, races, social classes, and ages. It is a problem in disadvantaged communities and among the homeless, and it is also a problem in rich neighborhoods and prestigious schools. The 2015 National Survey on Drug Use and Health found that 38 percent of American adults had taken prescription opioids in the last year. About 5 percent had misused prescription opioids by not taking them as prescribed. Two million Americans, about 1 percent of the population over the age of twelve,

Counterfeit Pills and the Death of Prince

Prince died in 2016 after overdosing on fentanyl.

Whenever drugs are bought on the street, there is a chance they contain fentanyl. There have even been cases of non-opioid drugs, like cocaine and marijuana, containing fentanyl. Even when a drug appears to be a prescription pill— that should contain a specific amount of a drug—it can always be a counterfeit. Since the effective dose of fentanyl is about the size a grain of sand, counterfeit pills may contain too much fentanyl by accident. The smallest mistake in the production of street drugs can cost someone their life.

This is what happened to music superstar Prince. The iconic singer was addicted to counterfeit pharmaceuticals that contained fentanyl. He took them for chronic pain. According to his inner circle, Prince was worried that if he got a prescription for opioids the news would leak to the press. Instead, he bought what he thought were prescription pills from a dealer.

After an overdose, Prince's friends talked to an addiction specialist. The rehab center sent over someone to talk to Prince about seeking help for his addiction. Tragically, the rehab center representative found Prince unresponsive when he arrived. Paramedics could not revive Prince, and he was pronounced dead. The cause of death was determined to be a fentanyl overdose.

had opioid use disorder. This is the medical term for someone with a "problematic pattern of opioid use leading to clinically significant impairment or distress" according to the *DSM-5*.

Although there is no typical opioid user, there are some patterns. Most people who misuse opioids first misuse prescription opioids. Sometimes, they misuse their own prescription, taking more than they are prescribed. Other times, they misuse prescription pills of a family member or a friend. They may be given the pills, or they may take them from an old prescription forgotten in the bathroom cabinet. This is why it is so important to dispose of leftover prescription pills.

At first, it is possible to take opioids infrequently without becoming dependent on them. Many people misuse opioids occasionally and do not find it hard to stop taking them. Yet with continued misuse, dependence occurs. Dependence means that when a person stops taking opioids, they experience unpleasant symptoms like anxiety, difficulty sleeping, muscle pain, and nausea. Taking more opioids relieves these symptoms for a short time.

When a person is dependent on opioids, a certain amount is needed every day just to stay well and prevent withdrawal. Much more is needed for any sort of high. As a person keeps trying to chase the high they used to experience, more and more opioids are taken. This cycle quickly becomes expensive. Life needs to be organized around acquiring and taking opioids multiple times a day just to keep functioning.

The average age of someone who misuses prescription opioids for the first time is about twenty-one years old. People between the ages of eighteen and twenty-five are the most likely to misuse opioids. Nonetheless, many people younger than this misuse opioids. In 2016, an estimated 239,000 adolescents between the ages of twelve and seventeen misused opioids. That is 1 percent of Americans in this age group.

Most people who misuse opioids begin by taking them orally, which means swallowing them. It is the intended way for prescription pills and syrups to be taken. Many people begin taking opioids in different ways as time goes on. At first, this is often done intranasally, or by snorting the drug. Intranasal use increases the effect of the drug but also makes overdose more likely.

Some people then go on to inject opioids. Injecting opioids increases the strength of a dose, and users can get high on less of the drug. Very few people who use opioids begin by injecting them. It is usually only when they are addicted that they are forced to inject the drug to cut down on how much they need to buy. Injecting opioids not only greatly increases the risk of overdose, it also comes with many other health risks like HIV/AIDS.

The same reason that people begin injecting the drug—to cut costs—is also why most heroin users first use heroin. Four out of five heroin users previously misused prescription opioids. Eventually, they cannot afford to buy enough prescription opioids to get high. This is the point when many people turn to heroin. According to a 2016 survey, 94 percent of heroin users said they only used the drug because it was cheaper or easier to find than prescription opioids.

Though heroin is cheaper than prescription opioids, its use is more dangerous. Heroin is often injected. However, many users begin by snorting or smoking it. Regardless of how it is taken, there is a risk of overdose, especially if the heroin contains fentanyl.

Approximately 0.2 percent of Americans above the age of twelve have used heroin in the past month, according to the National Survey of Drug Use and Health in 2017. This is about half a million people. The number has likely grown since the survey, as the number of overdoses has increased dramatically since 2017.

SIGNS OF OPIOID ADDICTION

There are many warning signs of opioid use disorder. If you are unsure if a person is taking opioids, there are some physical signs of use. These include trouble staying awake, flushed and itchy skin, and confusion. If you are taking prescription opioids for pain, these are signs that you may be taking too much. You should check with your prescribing doctor that the dosage is appropriate.

Pinned pupils are another sign of opioid use. Usually, a person's pupils respond to how light it is in their surroundings. In a dark environment, pupils rapidly expand to be quite large. In a bright environment, they contract to become small. This is the body's natural reaction to light. When using

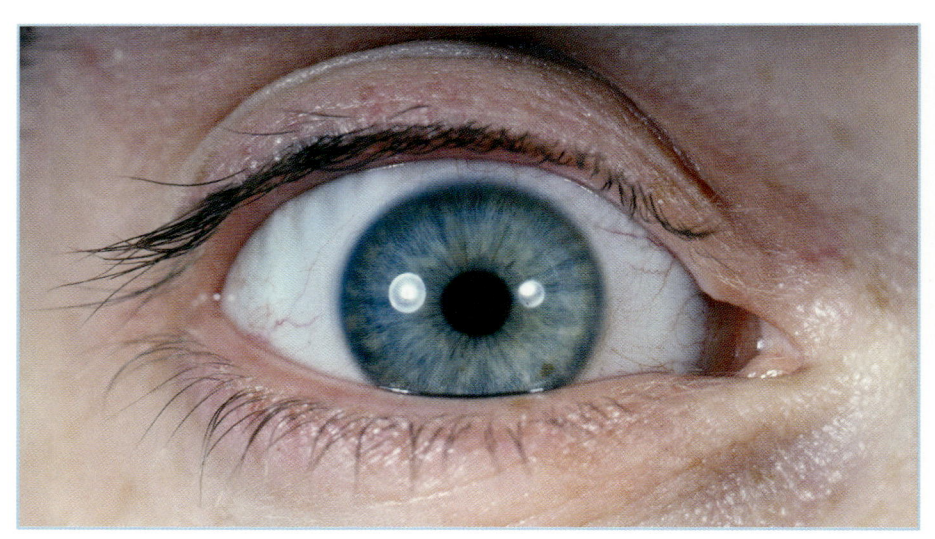

Pinned pupils, or pupils that stay small even in bright light, can be a sign of opioid use.

opioids, a person's pupils tend to be pinned—or quite small—all the time. They do not respond to light. This is one thing that paramedics and police officers are checking for when they shine a light into a person's eyes.

While the physical signs of opioid use are straightforward, determining whether prescribed opioids are being misused can be quite difficult. Doctors look at many different issues when trying to figure out if a patient is misusing opioids. There is rarely an easy way to tell if someone is struggling with opioid use disorder. Not taking opioids as directed is a red flag, but it is not enough to diagnose an opioid use disorder on its own.

Another major warning sign is when a person repeatedly tries to get prescribed more opioids. They report "losing" prescriptions and needing new ones as a result. They may also go the emergency room—or another doctor—to get more prescription opioids.

Trying unsuccessfully to cut back on opioids is another warning sign of opioid use disorder. If you are

Myth: Addiction Is a Lack of Willpower

One myth about opioid addiction is that people who misuse opioids simply lack the willpower to quit. This is not the case. Addiction is a medical issue with legitimate causes. Risk factors like genetics make someone likely to become addicted. Addiction then changes the way that the brain works, making it difficult for someone to quit. Opioid addiction also involves the intense physical and psychological suffering of withdrawal.

The National Institute on Alcohol Abuse and Alcoholism is based at the National Institutes of Health in Bethesda, Maryland.

Experts agree on all of these points. According to Dr. George Koob, director of NIH's National Institute on Alcohol Abuse and Alcoholism:

> **A common misperception is that addiction is a choice or moral problem, and all you have to do is stop. But nothing could be further from the truth. The brain actually changes with addiction, and it takes a good deal of work to get it back to its normal state. The more drugs or alcohol you've taken, the more disruptive it is to the brain.**

To recover, people who misuse opioids need more than just willpower. They need medical treatment and support. It is still likely they will relapse at least once. Yet with continued help, recovery is possible.

worried you may have a problem with your prescribed opioids, this is a symptom you should think about. If you have tried to cut back and failed, it is a sign you may need help. However, it does not always indicate a problem. If the difficulty cutting back relates to the pain the opioids were prescribed to treat, struggling may well be expected.

If you are concerned that you have a problem, you should talk your doctor. They can help you understand what to expect and what may be a problem when you are taking prescription opioids. If you are concerned that you have a problem with street drugs, you should talk to your doctor immediately. The earlier you seek help, the easier it will be to make changes that can prevent future difficulties.

THE STIGMA OF ADDICTION

If you or someone you know does have opioid use disorder, you should know that help is available. In chapter 4, we will look at the many treatment options that can help someone. It is important to remember that an opioid use disorder is a disease. It is treatable, and it should not be a source of shame.

Addiction is a medical issue and not a personal failing. People in the United States and around the world are coming to realize this more and more. Many organizations are fighting for the rights of people suffering from addiction and trying to change old, outdated attitudes toward addiction. Stigmatization—societal disapproval—just makes things more difficult for people struggling with opioid misuse.

It is important to get help—or encourage someone else to get help—for an opioid use disorder. Getting help is more important than worrying about social stigma. Opioid use disorder will not get better on its own, and effective treatments can make the journey to recovery much easier.

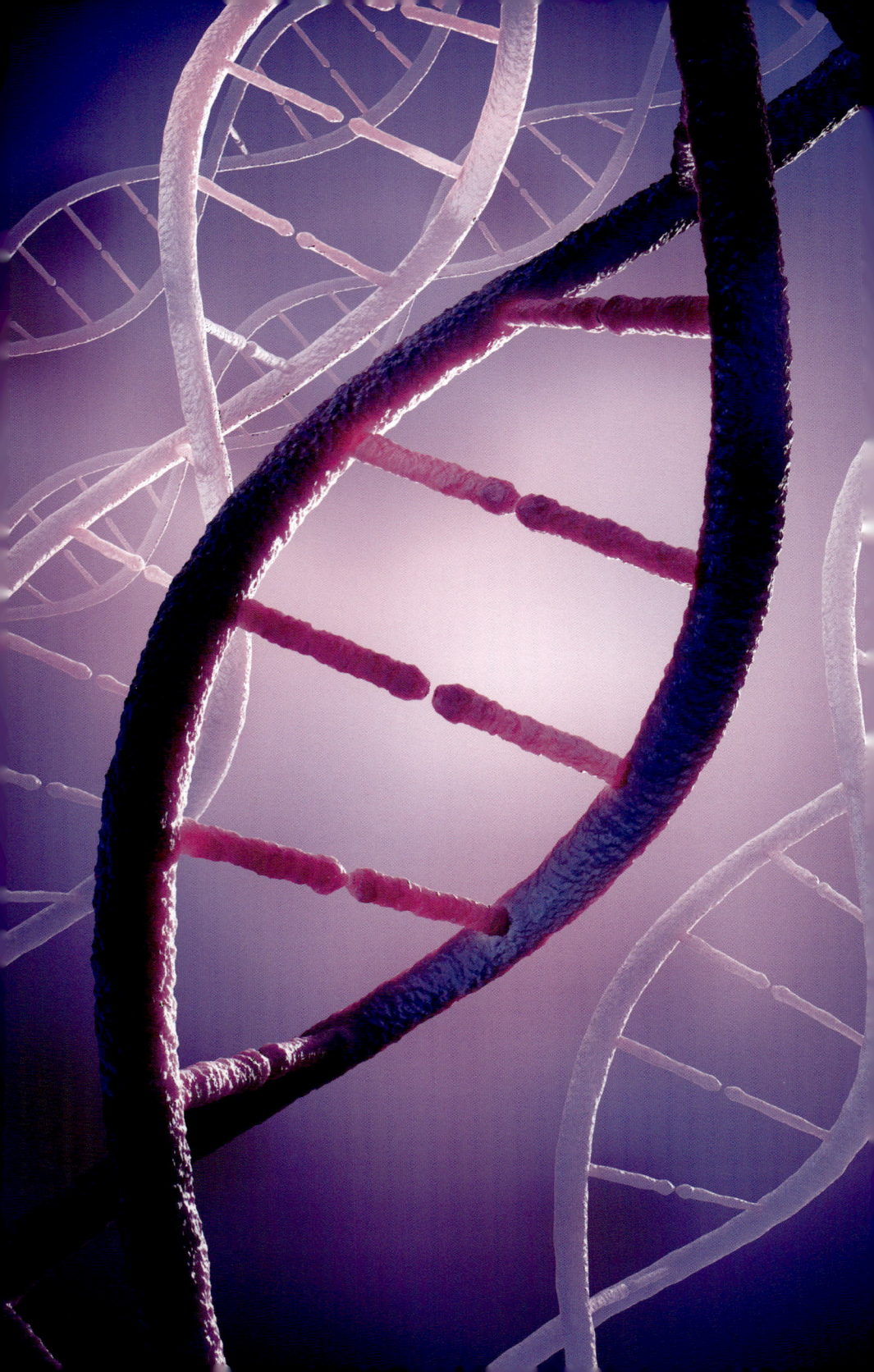

Chapter 2

Risk Factors of Opioid Misuse

While opioid use disorder (OUD) is a problem that can affect anyone, some people are at higher risk. In this chapter, we will look at the many risk factors that increase the odds of OUD. None of these risk factors make it certain that a person will develop OUD. However, someone who is at risk should be careful when using prescribed opioids. It is important to remember risk is not about willpower. According to Dr. Henry Kranzler, "Risk is not about character. It's about genetics and

Opposite: Genetics are one major risk factor for opioid use disorder.

environmental exposure." While we cannot change our genetics, we can shape our environment.

UNDERSTANDING RISK

In 2015, more than one-third of American adults were prescribed opioids. Opioids are prescribed for all sorts of reasons, from injury to surgery to chronic pain. Often, the prescription is a one-time thing, given after a tooth is pulled or a bone is broken. Sometimes, opioids are prescribed for chronic pain, and patients are given a prescription that can be refilled. A small percentage of opioids are given to the terminally ill, to make their last days more comfortable. In the case of the terminally ill, there is little worry about tolerance, withdrawal, and addiction.

Of the more than ninety million Americans prescribed opioids in 2015, most did not develop OUD. Researchers have spent a great deal of time and effort trying to figure out why some people do develop OUD and others do not. Through scientific studies, they have found many risk factors. These are circumstances that make it much more likely for a person to develop OUD, and they include but are not limited to genetics, environmental factors, and trauma.

GENETICS

The most important risk factor for opioid use disorder is genetics. According to studies, between 40 and 60 percent of a person's risk of developing OUD comes down to their genes. Scientists have pinpointed more than a hundred genes that influence a person's vulnerability to opioid addiction. Some genes increase a person's risk of developing drug addiction to any number of drugs, not just opioids. Others are specific to opioid addiction. For instance, some genes affect how a person's opioid receptors work in their brain. This puts some people at higher risk of developing OUD.

You cannot know for certain if you have genetic risk factors for OUD. However, if there is a history of addiction, especially drug and opioid addiction, in your family, genes might play a role. A family history of addiction is a good reason to be wary of taking prescription opioids unless necessary. It is also a good reason to think twice about taking opioids recreationally again if you have done so in the past.

Currently, scientists are hoping that genetic testing may someday improve treatment options for opioid use disorder. There is some evidence that certain treatments are more effective for people based on their genetics. Ongoing research in this area may one day help people who misuse opioids to recover.

ENVIRONMENTAL FACTORS

Genetics explain about half of a person's risk of developing OUD. The other half is explained by environmental factors. Environmental factors relate to our environment—or the world around us. There are a number of environmental risk factors that may come from any aspect of a person's life, from their home and family to their school and friends. These risk factors never cause OUD by themselves. For instance, some people who are exposed to opioids at a young age swear never to use them. However, when scientists look at all the people who misuse opioids, the following environmental factors put people at a higher risk of developing OUD.

Home Environment

If someone in a person's home misuses opioids, it is an environmental risk factor. It puts an individual at a much higher risk of developing OUD. It may be a person's parents or siblings who misuse opioids or a member of their extended family. In fact, any drug or alcohol misuse in the home increases a person's risk of every kind of drug addiction, including opioid addiction. The risk for OUD in particular is even higher when a family member misuses opioids rather than another substance. Their opioid use introduces the idea that opioids can be misused. It may also normalize opioid misuse if a person sees it in their home.

One friend's opioid misuse can make it more likely that others around them will misuse drugs.

Peer Pressure

If someone's friends or peers misuse opioids, it also makes OUD more likely. Seeing a friend misuse opioids makes it seem more normal than it otherwise would be. Furthermore, a person whose friends misuse opioids may be subjected to peer pressure to misuse them as well.

Peer pressure can take many forms. It can occur when friends actively encourage someone to take opioids. It can also be a feeling. A person may feel left out when their friends are taking opioids and they are not, even if their friends do not encourage them to do it.

ACCESS TO OPIOIDS

One important environmental risk factor is simple: access to opioids. Opioids are a controlled substance. They require a prescription to have them legally. Street drugs like heroin must be bought illegally—

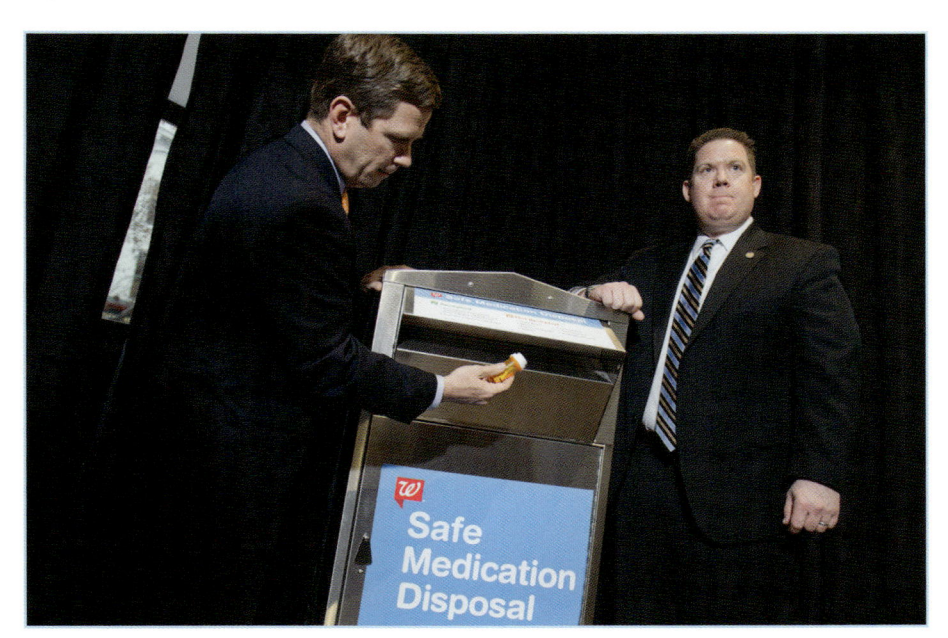

Two politicians unveil a safe medication disposal kiosk designed to help communities fight opioid misuse by making sure old medication isn't misused.

"Hey Charlie"

Many organizations are trying to slow the spread of the opioid epidemic. From government agencies to nonprofits, many groups try to warn potential new users not to start misusing opioids or to quit if they've already begun.

Some of these groups partnered to produce a video in 2018 that highlights the dangers of opioid misuse. Called "Hey Charlie," it follows a fictional teen character, Charlie, who gets hooked on opioids. He quickly goes from being an athlete and good student to struggling with the effects of OUD.

"Hey Charlie" is noteworthy because it was also written by a teen, Brinkley Smithers. She volunteered at the Long Island Council on Alcohol and Drug Dependence (LICADD). After seeing the struggle of people misusing opioids first-hand, she wanted to help and do more to combat the stigma of opioid misuse. Smithers came up with the idea for the video, and the Christopher D. Smithers Foundation, founded by her grandfather, helped make it a reality.

Smithers later explained how she imagined the main character, Charlie, "I wanted to make it like it could be any other normal kid that you just would imagine, who's doing well; he just fell into the wrong thing at the wrong time at a party— how it usually kind of happens." The video is available online at http://www.stopthespiral.com.

#StopTheSpiral is a collaborative project between the Christopher D. Smithers Foundation and the Columbia University Medical Center. It aims to end the opioid epidemic and expand treatment options for those struggling with OUD.

something that is often difficult, dangerous, and risky. Sometimes, easy access overlaps with family and friend misuse. They may provide opioids. Other times, access to opioids may be as simple as an old prescription that is lying around. It can also include your own prescription opioids from a doctor.

If you are worried about opioid misuse by yourself or others, this is one of the easiest risk factors to control. Prescription opioids that are not being used should be disposed of safely and not abandoned in a medicine cabinet. You can talk to your family to make sure this is the case in your household.

EARLY USE

The younger a person is when they begin using opioids, the more likely they are to develop OUD. There are many reasons for this. Scientists believe it may have to do with the fact that young children who get their hands on opioids are likely to have other risk factors as well. Additionally, the effect of opioids on the brain may be greater on young users. The brain does not finish developing until the mid-twenties. This means teens who take opioids experience greater changes in their brains than adults do.

Opioids alter the way that the brain works as well as its structure. Scientists can measure physical changes in the brain from opioid use by using brain scans. They have found that opioid use affects parts of the brain that manage self-control, emotions, and pleasure. The ability to resist impulses, like using more opioids, decreases. Managing emotions and stress also becomes more difficult without using opioids once someone is accustomed to them.

STRESS AND TRAUMA

High levels of stress are another risk factor for OUD. People under chronic stress are much more likely to seek out more opioids after first using them. Additionally, stress is a major risk factor for relapse. Once a person with OUD has quit using opioids, periods of high stress make it more likely they will start again.

One in six American children experiences hunger on a routine basis. Hunger is one example of stress or trauma that can increase the likelihood of opioid and other drug use.

Stress can result from all sorts of situations. It may be due to a person's home, school, or work environment. Too much work and too little sleep cause stress. Events, like the death of a loved one, can be very stressful. Stress can also be due to physical causes. Hunger is a common stressor for children and teens. While we may think of hunger as a problem that affects other countries and not the

United States or Canada, this is not the case. One in six children in the United States does not have enough food to eat on a regular basis.

Trauma also puts people at risk for OUD. Emotional trauma results from having experienced a horrible event. Childhood traumas include abuse, neglect, and witnessing violence. Being the victim of assault or experiencing conflict as a soldier can also cause trauma. Past trauma puts a person at greater risk of addiction to any substance, including opioids, as well as other drugs and alcohol. However, it is important to remember that not everyone who experiences trauma will develop problems with drugs or alcohol. Additionally, many people with OUD have not experienced past trauma.

MENTAL ILLNESS

There is a complicated relationship between substance-use disorders (SUDs), including OUD, and mental illness. About one-half of people who experience mental illness will also experience an

About 50 percent of people with a substance use disorder have struggled with mental illness or will face problems with mental illness in the future.

SUD in their life. Likewise, half of people with an SUD experience mental illness either before, during, or after their SUD. The exact nature of the relationship between these two medical issues varies by the individual. Doctors are still studying how substance use and mental illness are related.

Mental illness is a broad term that covers many different disorders. SUDs are considered a mental illness. Like OUD, mental illnesses are disorders driven by genetics and characteristics of the brain, not a person's character. A person who experiences mental illness is not weak-willed or crazy. Mental illnesses include anxiety disorders, panic disorder, depression, bipolar disorder, schizophrenia, and post-traumatic stress disorder (PTSD). Sometimes, mental illness may interfere with daily activities. Other times, mental illness is not apparent in a person's behavior.

Sometimes, the relationship between SUDs and mental illness is quite direct. For example, smoking marijuana as an adolescent puts a person at higher risk of psychosis (a severe mental illness marked by losing touch with reality). This link between marijuana use and psychosis is tied to a specific gene. It does not affect most people.

Usually, the relationship between SUDs and mental illness is indirect. A person may begin using drugs to manage symptoms of untreated mental illness. Drugs like opioids can initially reduce anxiety, before making the symptoms much worse. Likewise, stimulants are sometimes used to treat undiagnosed ADHD (attention deficit hyperactive disorder). Treating undiagnosed mental illness with illegal drugs is dangerous and should never be done.

Many of the risk factors of SUDs and mental illness are the same: stress, trauma, and genes. It is often hard to see exactly how SUDs and mental illness affect each other in a specific case. Yet there is no doubt that mental illness and SUDs (including OUD) are a major risk factor for each other.

OVERDOSE RISK FACTORS

Just as there are risk factors for OUD, there are also risk factors for opioid overdose. Opioids affect how the brain regulates breathing. When a person takes too much, their breathing weakens to the point that death may result. This is an opioid overdose. In addition to death from respiratory depression, sometimes people die from other symptoms. Inhaling and choking to death on vomit is a possible cause of death as well.

Overdoses most often occur when opioids are misused and not taken as prescribed. However, occasionally patients do overdose when taking medications as prescribed. This can sometimes occur when opioids are mixed with other medications, although it is rare, since a person's doctor and pharmacist should both catch these interactions.

Mixing medications, especially medications that are not prescribed to you, can cause serious health problems and even an overdose.

Mixing Drugs

Mixing drugs is one of the greatest risk factors of a drug overdose. This is why doctors and pharmacists are aware of, and on the lookout for, possible drug interactions. Opioids are not the only drug that depress breathing. Sedatives and alcohol do the same. When these drugs are mixed with opioids, the chance of overdose and death are much higher than when these drugs are used alone. In fact, more than half of fatal overdoses in the United States involve more than one drug.

According to studies, seven out of ten teens who take opioids for nonmedical purposes mix them with other drugs. This is an extraordinarily high number, given the risks involved. Mixing alcohol and opioids can turn a less-than-fatal amount of either one into a deadly cocktail.

Sedatives, especially benzodiazepines like Xanax and Valium, are also commonly mixed and exceptionally dangerous when used with opioids. The combined effect of both drugs on a person's breathing is much greater than either drug in isolation. Respiratory depression can make a person go unconscious without warning. Unless someone else very quickly gets them medical aid, death may result.

Arrests and Incarceration

Another risk factor for opioid overdose is a history of arrests or incarceration (serving time in jail or prison). Often, these arrests may be for possession of opioids.

A person's tolerance for a drug can change while they are behind bars. This can lead them to overdose when released, due to misjudged dosages.

What's in a Name?

The term "opioid use disorder" (OUD) only became widespread in 2013. That year, the fifth edition of the *Diagnostic and Statistical Manual of Mental Disorders* (*DSM-5*) was published. This is the manual that mental health professionals use to diagnose disorders. Previously, "opioid dependence" and "opioid abuse" were used instead.

In the new edition of the *DSM*, treating opioid use disorder as these two separate disorders— opioid dependence and abuse— was judged as incorrect. It led to problems where people who misused opioids did not quite meet either criteria, and it did not make diagnosis or treatment easier. That is why "OUD" is now used instead.

DSM-5 lists eleven criteria for OUD. They include taking more opioids than prescribed, strong cravings for opioids, unsuccessful attempts to cut down on use, and using opioids despite the fact that they contribute to professional, personal, or social problems. *DSM-5* also lists tolerance— needing to take more opioids for the same effect— and withdrawal symptoms when stopping opioids as criteria for OUD. (It is important to note that these last two are not considered evidence of OUD in people who take prescription opioids as directed. Tolerance and withdrawal are expected in long-term opioid use for pain relief.) The more of these criteria a person meets, the more severe the case of OUD.

A separate issue is that the term "opioid abuse" is currently falling out of favor. Professionals worry the term carries too much stigma. It comes with negative perceptions of people who misuse opioids. As a result, "opioid misuse" is being used more and more frequently instead of "opioid abuse."

It is important to note that possessing opioids is almost always illegal, unless they are prescribed to you. Even if they are prescription opioids, it is illegal to have them unless they are in a prescription bottle with your name on it. In many states, it is possible to receive a sentence of many years in prison for possessing not only heroin, but also prescription pills like OxyContin. As a result, long-term opioid users often have a criminal history and have served time in jail or prison.

Serving time then becomes a major risk factor for overdose. There is little a person can do to change this risk factor since it is based on their past. However, a person with a history of misusing opioids needs to be careful when they are released from prison or jail. This is when people are at the highest risk of overdosing on opioids. Their tolerance to opioids—how much they can take before overdosing—is extremely low if they were not taking opioids in prison. Upon being released, a person can mistakenly believe their tolerance is similar to what it was before they served time and take too much. Studies show that someone is three to eight times more likely to die from a drug overdose within two weeks of being released from prison.

THERE IS HOPE

No matter how many risk factors a person has, there is no guarantee they will develop OUD. Many people have risk factors and never misuse opioids. If you do you have risk factors, it is good to be aware of them. You may want to discuss any concerns with a doctor if they want to prescribe you opioids.

It is also important to remember that opioid use disorder is a disease that can be treated. If you or someone you know has a problem, there is help available. You can stop using opioids. There are many treatments available that make quitting easier than it may seem on your own.

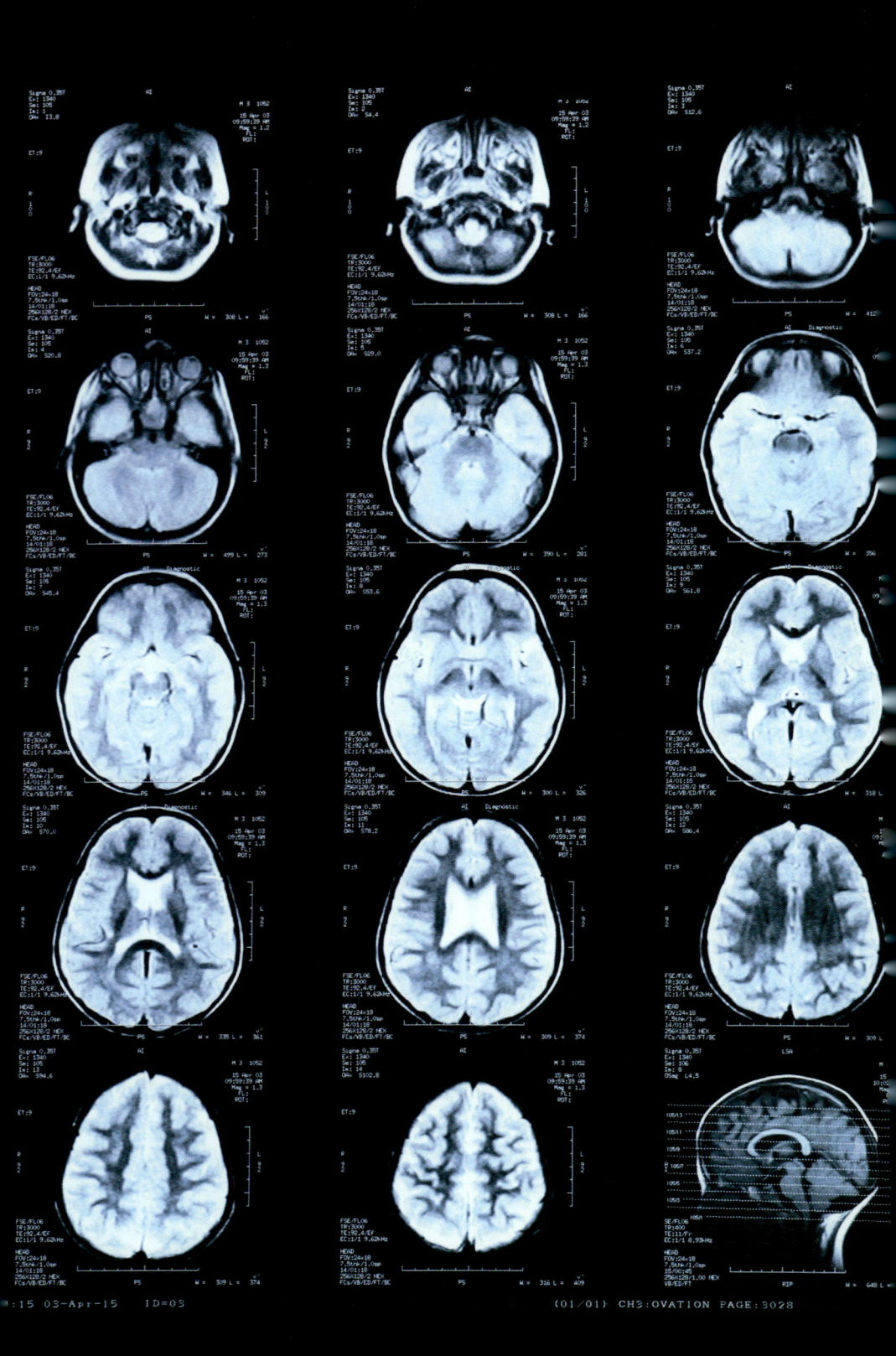

Chapter 3

Experiencing Opioid Misuse

Everyone's experience with opioid misuse is different. Some people only ever misuse opioids that doctors prescribe them. Other people misuse prescription opioids that they obtain illegally or only take street drugs like heroin. Their experiences may be different when it comes to issues like social stigma, health risks, and day-to-day challenges. At the same time, many people's experiences with opioid

Opposite: Drug use causes structural changes in the brain. Young brains that are still forming (shown here) are especially vulnerable.

misuse have similarities. With frequent opioid use, they will develop a higher tolerance to opioids and eventually suffer through withdrawal symptoms when they try to stop using opioids.

OPIOID TOLERANCE

As a person uses opioids, the drugs become less and less effective. This applies to both their painkilling effect when taken for medical reasons and their

Narcan nasal spray can reverse overdoses. EMTs and members of law enforcement often carry Narcan.

euphoric effect when taken recreationally. The brain adapts to the presence of opioids, and larger and larger doses are needed to obtain the same result.

As a person takes more and more opioids, the side effects increase as well. These include drowsiness, nausea, and constipation. These side effects plague both people who take opioids as prescribed for pain and people who misuse opioids. At high doses, the side effects of opioids can be difficult to manage.

As a person's tolerance increases and they take more opioids, the amount required to overdose increases. People who frequently misuse opioids often take what would be a lethal amount in someone with no tolerance. Despite this increase in tolerance, overdose is a very real possibility for long-term opioid users. Luckily, overdoses can be reversed if someone receives medical aid quickly.

Narcan is used to reverse an opioid overdose. It is an opioid antagonist. This means it binds with opioid receptors in the brain, stripping away opioid agonists like heroin or oxycodone that are there during an overdose. Stripping away opioid agonists reverses the respiratory depression that causes unconsciousness and death during an overdose.

WITHDRAWAL SYMPTOMS

Withdrawal symptoms occur when someone who is dependent on opioids stops using them. This

A nurse readies methadone at a health-care center. Methadone can ease withdrawal symptoms when it's administered by a professional.

includes both people who misuse them and people who take them as prescribed over a long period of time. The amount of time between a person's last dose of opioids and the onset of symptoms varies according to a number of factors. The most important factor is which opioid the person is using. For the most commonly misused opioids, like OxyContin and heroin, withdrawal symptoms occur about twelve hours after the last dose. People who misuse OxyContin and heroin take them at least two or three times a day. Some opioids, like methadone, last much longer. Methadone can stave off withdrawal symptoms for about a day.

Symptoms of withdrawal vary in intensity depending on how severe someone's dependence is and how long they have taken opioids. The more a person takes, and the longer they have regularly taken opioids, the worse their symptoms. This is a good reason to try to quit opioids sooner rather than later.

Typical symptoms of withdrawal are both physical and psychological. Physical symptoms include goose bumps, runny nose, teary eyes, sneezing, and bodily aches and pains. The digestive system is also affected; diarrhea, cramps, nausea, and vomiting can occur. Psychological symptoms include anxiety, restlessness, irritability, difficulty sleeping, and intense cravings for opioids.

Symptoms of withdrawal for relatively short-acting opioids like heroin, Vicodin, or oxycodone last about a week. Withdrawal from methadone can last longer. Withdrawal from opioids is quite unpleasant, but it's rarely dangerous. Death is very unusual, and most recorded instances have been in settings like prison, where a person was refused medical aid.

Once a person is dependent on opioids, opioids begin to rule their life. They are forced to take opioids multiple times a day to avoid the miserable experience of withdrawal. If they have a prescription and misuse it, this often results in them running out of pills early. If they buy opioids illegally, it means constantly trying to gather enough money to go buy opioids. Constant worry about how to obtain opioids and preventing withdrawal are an experience that most people who misuse opioids talk about.

DANGEROUS ADDITIVES

Prescription opioids are not safe to misuse, and street opioids are never safe to use. The risks of addiction, overdose, and side effects are the same for both. Additionally, each carries unique risks of their own. These risks are due to substances outside of the opioids themselves.

Heroin and fake prescription pills may contain all sorts of adulterants, which are added to reduce the purity and make selling drugs more profitable. Common adulterants include sugar, baking soda, and crushed over-the-counter tablets. However, sometimes extremely dangerous adulterants are used. Heroin has tested positive for substances like rat poison and laundry detergent. Consuming these adulterants can put your health at risk.

While the contents of prescription pills may be known, they can still contain dangerous substances. Many prescription pills contain large amounts of acetaminophen (the active ingredient in Tylenol). Acetaminophen increases the painkilling effect of opioids when the pills are used properly. However, many people with opioid use disorder take more pills than they should. When more than the recommended dose is taken, acetaminophen can be extremely dangerous. Overdoses cause liver damage.

In high enough doses, acetaminophen causes liver failure and death. It is the leading cause of acute liver failure in the United States, and more than five hundred people die from acetaminophen overdose each year. People who misuse prescription opioids that contain acetaminophen, like Vicodin and Percocet, are at greater risk of accidental acetaminophen overdose. It is critically important for users of these drugs to be aware of the maximum recommended dose of acetaminophen as well as how much the pills they are taking contain.

Other prescription opioids have risks associated with injecting them. In recent years, pharmaceutical companies have tried to prevent the misuse of their medications. One way they have tried to prevent misuse is to make some pills difficult to crush or dissolve in water. This makes them difficult to snort or inject. Some pills contain additives that make them turn into gel on contact with water.

In theory, these measures prevent people from injecting the contents of pills. Unfortunately, this is not always the case. Although it is difficult and wastes much of the pill, some people still inject these "abuse-proof" formulations. This can have terrible consequences for their health, since the resulting mixture is tainted with the tamper-resistant additives. These additives can damage a person's blood vessels. One possible complication is thrombotic

Harm Reduction

Protesters gather in Washington, DC, to ask Congress to enact harm reduction measures.

In the world of addiction treatment, "harm reduction" is a controversial phrase. It refers to efforts to limit the harm from drug use. Harm reduction often seeks to limit the number of deaths from overdose as well as prevent the spread of diseases like HIV/AIDS. At first glance, it is hard to see how this could be controversial. However, in the United States, harm-reduction programs have a history of being stopped by the federal government in Washington, DC.

According to researcher Don C. Des Jarlais, the controversy surrounding harm reduction is due to the stigmatization and demonization of drug use in American society. Des Jarlais notes the "demonization of specific drugs did not prevent the use of the drugs, but it did create a context in which the drugs were feared, there was fear of and anger toward the drug users, and abstinence was seen as the only acceptable policy towards drug use." Abstinence means not taking a drug. Opponents of harm reduction tend to believe in abstinence-only policies. They see harm reduction as making it easier for people to use drugs.

On the other hand, almost all scientists and doctors support harm reduction. It is a proven, cheap way to reduce deaths and disease. One method of harm reduction is needle exchanges. Needle exchanges are places where people who inject drugs can trade in used needles for new ones, preventing them from having to share needles. Needle exchanges have been shown to lower rates of HIV/AIDS. Other harm reduction measures include distributing Narcan and staffing safe-injection sites where people can use drugs with medical supervision. Both have reduced overdoses in countries around the world and prevented many deaths.

microangiopathy (TMA). TMA results from blood clots lodging in small blood vessels throughout the body and damaging them. It is a life-threatening condition that can cause liver damage, visual impairment, and stomach pain.

THE DANGERS OF INJECTING DRUGS

Injecting drugs is always dangerous. Even under the best of circumstances with new, sterile equipment in a hospital, it comes with risks. Injecting opioids outside of a hospital is even more dangerous. It is possible to minimize the risk of some of these issues, but again, it is never safe to inject drugs. This overview will cover some of the most common health problems that result from injecting drugs. There are other complications that can occur as well.

HIV/AIDS

The human immunodeficiency virus (HIV) is spread through bodily fluids such as blood. Over time, HIV

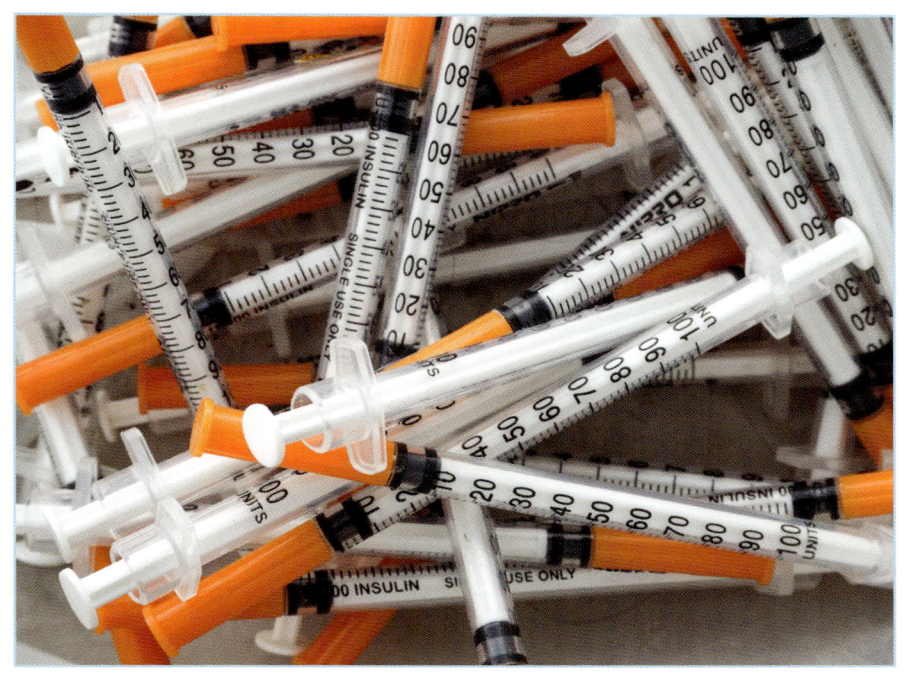

Injecting drugs is always risky. Consequences include contracting HIV and hepatitis C.

infection can lead to acquired immunodeficiency syndrome (AIDS). In other words, HIV refers to the virus that causes HIV infection. AIDS refers to a collection of symptoms that occur in the later stages of an HIV infection. AIDS can usually be prevented in people living with HIV if they receive treatment.

Injecting drugs puts a person at risk for HIV/AIDS. The virus can live outside the human body in needles and other injection equipment in microscopic amounts of blood. If these are shared, the disease can spread.

The Center for Disease Control (CDC) estimates that between 6 and 9 percent of new HIV infections in 2015 were the result of injecting drugs. If that rate continues, the CDC estimates "1 in 23 women who inject drugs and 1 in 36 men who inject drugs will be diagnosed with HIV in their lifetime."

Many people living with HIV are unaware of the fact that they've contracted the virus. This lack of awareness is a major problem because it prevents treatment. Without treatment, HIV leads to AIDS in approximately ten years. If someone with AIDS is still not treated, average life expectancy is just three years. Fortunately, with treatment, someone living with HIV has the same life expectancy as their peers not living with HIV. Treatment options are highly effective today.

Hepatitis C

Hepatitis C is another bloodborne virus that is spread through injecting drugs. Injecting drugs is responsible for more than half of new hepatitis C cases in the United States each year. Unlike HIV, hepatitis C can even be transmitted through sharing equipment used for snorting drugs, such as straws or rolled-up bills.

The word "hepatitis" means inflammation of the liver. Hepatitis C is a specific virus that causes hepatitis. The hepatitis C virus (HCV) causes both acute infections and chronic infections. Acute infections are short-lived, while chronic infections do not go away. About one-third of people with acute infections will fully recover without developing a chronic infection. Many of them will never even know they were infected due to a lack of symptoms. Unfortunately, about two-thirds of hepatitis C cases develop into a chronic HCV infection. This is an extremely serious condition that can lead to liver damage and death.

Chronic HCV infection can cause cirrhosis of the liver. Cirrhosis is permanent scarring of the liver. It causes decreased liver function. There are often no symptoms in the early stages of cirrhosis. Then, as the condition worsens, life-threatening complications can occur as the liver stops being able to perform its function.

If you have injected drugs or shared snorting equipment, it is important to get tested for hepatitis C infection. Many people show no symptoms of an infection. However, the virus may be damaging their liver. If the disease is caught early, outcomes are very good. About 95 percent of the time, patients can be cured. This means that the virus can no longer be detected in a patient's blood three months after completing treatment. At this point, the virus rarely reoccurs. However, when a person is cured, it does not mean they are immune to the HCV. If they continue to inject drugs, they may get infected again.

While people who inject drugs are at a much greater risk for HIV and HCV infection, they can reduce their risk. The most effective way to do this is to never share needles and related equipment with other people. This includes equipment like cookers (used to heat the drug), cottons (or other filters), and water. Blood can contaminate any of these things and spread diseases—even if the amount is too little to see with the naked eye.

Abscesses

Abscesses frequently result from injecting drugs. They are collections of pus under the skin that can open, creating a sore or ulcer as well. They are often hard to touch and form a raised bump or knot under the skin. Abscesses may also be hot or painful when touched.

Most abscesses are infections from bacteria that live on the skin. When injecting drugs, these bacteria are introduced into the body. The risk of abscesses can be reduced by cleaning the injection site with an alcohol pad. Using needles only one time and using sterile water can also reduce the chance of abscesses forming.

Abscesses can clear up on their own, but sometimes serious complications occur. It is important to get medical treatment for abscesses. If you or someone you know has an abscess, you should make sure they receive medical treatment. A doctor or nurse can safely treat the infection so that it does not spread or get worse. You should never try to lance or drain an abscess on your own.

If left untreated, abscesses can spread to the bone or lead to gangrene—the death of surrounding tissue. Complications like this can ultimately lead to amputation or death. For many people who inject drugs, abscesses are a frequent occurrence. Their frequency can lead to overconfidence that all abscesses will clear up on their own. In reality, it is always important to seek medical treatment for abscesses because they can result in extremely serious complications.

Collapsed Veins

Frequent injections, especially with used needles and unsterile equipment, can lead to collapsed veins. When veins are damaged repeatedly, the sides can heal together, effectively closing the vein completely. This makes it impossible to inject into the vein and impossible for blood to flow through it.

Usually, blood is pumped through smaller veins in the body once a major vein collapses. Sometimes, this blood flow may be insufficient to keep the body supplied with oxygen, causing circulation problems. Numbness and tingling in the extremities may become normal.

Collapsed veins can also force people who inject drugs to turn to other areas for injection sites. Typically, people begin injecting drugs into their arms before moving to their legs, hands, and feet. Once collapsed veins and scarring make these areas difficult to inject into, other locations are sometimes used. The veins in the groin and neck are especially dangerous. It is never worth the risk of injecting in these sites.

Deep Vein Thrombosis

Injecting drugs, especially into the groin, increases a person's risk for deep vein thrombosis (DVT). DVT occurs when a blood clot forms in a deep vein, typically in the legs. There are many risk factors for DVT. It is not always caused by injecting drugs, but injecting drugs is a serious risk factor.

DVT can have life-threatening complications. Often, there are no symptoms of the blood clot in the leg, although sometimes there is pain, swelling, or redness. If the clot dislodges from the deep vein, it can travel to the lungs and cause a pulmonary embolism, which is when a blood vessel in the lungs is blocked. Pulmonary embolisms can be fatal. Symptoms include shortness of breath, chest pain, and coughing up blood.

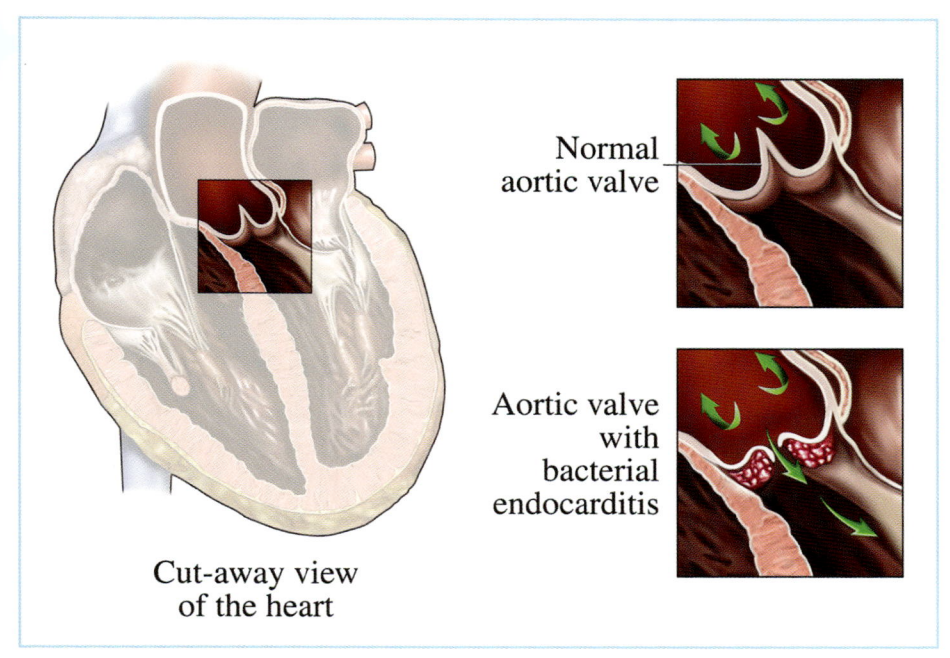

Normal
aortic valve

Aortic valve
with
bacterial
endocarditis

Cut-away view
of the heart

Endocarditis is an infection of the heart that is deadly if it is not treated.

Endocarditis

One of the most serious complications from injecting drugs is endocarditis. Endocarditis is an infection in the inner lining of the heart. Bacteria is introduced into the bloodstream when someone injects themselves. The bacteria can find their way to the heart and cause infection there. While not the only

Witnessing an Overdose

If someone near you is overdosing, it is essential that you call 911.

At some point in your life, you may witness an opioid overdose. It may be a friend or family member, or it could be a stranger. There are a number of signs of an opioid overdose. The person may be completely unresponsive or unable to talk. Trying to wake them up may not work. Their skin and lips may turn blue from lack of oxygen. Their breathing may be shallow or labored, like they cannot catch their breath. Sometimes, they may stop breathing. They may vomit or make gurgling noises.

If you see these symptoms, it is essential that you call 911 immediately. An opioid overdose is a life-threatening emergency, and the person may die without medical aid. If you have received training and have access to it, you may then administer Narcan. Narcan can be injectable or a nasal spray. Next, lay the person on their side and try to keep them awake while you wait for emergency services to respond. Opioid overdoses are surprisingly easy to reverse with Narcan— which paramedics carry. The main risk is that no one sees the person overdose, or the witness does not call 911.

Sometimes, people who see an opioid overdose are too scared of the police arresting someone to call 911. This fear is unfounded. Almost all states forbid the police from arresting people involved in an opioid overdose emergency. This is to encourage people to call 911 and save the life of the person overdosing.

cause of endocarditis, injecting drugs puts a person at a much greater risk of developing the condition.

Endocarditis can cause many symptoms, from weight loss to flu-like symptoms. It is often difficult to diagnose since these symptoms are not specific to the relatively rare condition. If a doctor knows a person injects drugs, it is much more likely they will test for it. However, many people who inject drugs hide this fact from their doctor due to social stigma and fear. If it is caught early, endocarditis can be treated with antibiotics and possibly surgery. If it worsens, it can cause death.

QUITTING OPIOIDS

It is never too late to stop misusing opioids. Many of the harmful effects will become much easier to treat or go away on their own once a person stops misusing opioids. Even infections with no cure, such as HIV, are manageable. The risk of most deadly problems, like acetaminophen overdose or endocarditis, disappears completely once a person quits.

While it is quite difficult to quit misusing opioids alone, it is much easier with help. There are medical options that make quitting easier. It is not a personal failing to seek help with an opioid addiction. It is the first step to getting better.

Chapter 4

Hope and Recovery

most people get sober and relapse multiple times before finally quitting opioids, but there is no shame in having to try more than once. The simple fact is that most people who misuse opioids do quit eventually. Today, there are more and better options to help someone quit opioids than ever before.

Opposite: Quitting opioids is an achievable goal. Never give up, and reach out when you need help.

GETTING HELP

If you have opioid use disorder or think that you might, there are people to turn to. If you are under the age of eighteen, the first step is to talk to a trusted adult. This is likely your parent or guardian. If they are not able or willing to help, it could also be a school counselor, coach, or teacher. Telling someone that you have a problem and need help is the beginning of your recovery. It takes a great deal of courage to admit you need help, and you should be proud of asking an adult for help.

With or without the help of a parent or guardian, you can talk to a doctor or addiction specialist. Your primary-care doctor is a good first option. They will be able to address your concerns and tell you about treatment options. They might also refer you to a specialist who knows more about OUD.

In the United States, what you tell your doctor is confidential. This mean they cannot tell your parents or law enforcement what you say to them. The one exception is if they have good reason to think you

Your doctor is there to help you fight opioid misuse. Make sure to tell him or her that you've been struggling.

will harm yourself or others. You should feel safe telling them the truth and sharing any concerns. However, your doctor will likely urge you to talk to your parents about your OUD if you have not already. You will need a parent's or guardian's permission for most treatment options if you are under the age of eighteen.

When you think of treatment, you might imagine a rehabilitation (rehab) facility that you live in. These are called inpatient rehabs. Patients stay there twenty-four hours a day. While this is an option, many people who recover from OUD never go to an inpatient rehab. Instead, they receive outpatient services. Outpatient rehabs treat patients who do not stay overnight. Patients simply come in for appointments and then leave. There is no reason to be scared of either inpatient or outpatient rehabs. You should not avoid treatment out of fear that you will be forced to live in a rehab facility.

Inpatient and outpatient rehabs come in many different varieties. Your doctor will know what is available in your area and which ones are affordable for your health insurance or for a person with no insurance. Rehabs usually offer many different types of help. Doctors at rehab will help you manage symptoms of withdrawal from opioids if you are physically dependent on them. This is called detoxification or detox. Rehabs also offer counseling and support during recovery.

HELPING OTHERS

If you think a friend or family member is misusing opioids, the first step is to talk to them about your concerns. Even if you are quite sure they have a problem, they may deny it. This is normal. You can

There are many ways to help a loved one who is misusing opioids, including listening to what they're going through.

Helplines

Helplines can give you information and guidance about opioid misuse.

If you or someone you know needs help with opioid misuse, help is just a phone call away. In the United States, you can call the Substance Abuse and Mental Health Services Administration (SAMHSA) National Helpline at 1-800-662-HELP (4357). Someone is ready to answer your call and provide assistance twenty-four hours a day.

A call to the SAMHSA National Helpline is confidential. They will ask for your ZIP code so that they know where you need services. However, they do not ask your name, and they do not keep records about who called. An information specialist will be able to provide you with information about local services to help with opioid misuse, including support groups as well as medical options. If you do not have health insurance, they can help you look for options that are still free or affordable.

If you live in Canada, there is no national helpline, but there are helplines for each province. You can visit the following web page to find the phone number for your province: https://www.canada.ca/en/health-canada/services/substance-use/get-help/get-help-with-drug-abuse.html. They will help you find services near your home.

Even if you are not sure about quitting opioids right away, a phone call to these hotlines can be useful. You can learn about resources that may be helpful in the future. If you are worried about affordable help, they can tell you about options near you. Since they are confidential, there is no need to worry that your parents or school will find out.

tell them why you think they have a problem and that you are worried about them, though you should try to avoid shaming them.

If they are open to the idea that they have a problem, you can encourage them to tell a trusted adult or see a doctor—either their own physician or an addiction specialist. A doctor will be able to help figure out treatment options and diagnose opioid use disorder.

If they ask, you may even go see a doctor or specialist with them. Otherwise, you can just support them outside of treatment. Encourage them to seek help and do their best to stop misusing opioids. If they relapse, don't give up on them. Just being there for a friend or family member who is struggling is helpful.

Listening is another way you can help. Having a friend to confide in without judgment is a huge help. Often, people who have OUD feel like there is no one they can talk to about their problems since drug use is illegal and stigmatized. By being there for them if they want to talk, you can help and encourage them to get better.

MYTHS ABOUT ADDICTION

One major way to help yourself or others suffering from OUD is to be informed. There are many harmful myths when it comes to drug addiction. People often believe these myths because they have never heard differently. Unfortunately, these mistaken ideas can sometimes have terrible consequences.

Confrontational Interventions: More Harm than Good

Confrontational interventions are when family members and friends confront someone with a substance use disorder. Participants speak out about all the ways that a person's addiction has affected them negatively. The person is then urged to get treatment for their addiction.

There are many styles of intervention. Some are relatively kind, while others try to shame and humiliate a person into seeking help. There is no evidence that focusing on bad things a person has done as a result of their addiction makes them more likely to get treatment. The reality TV show *Intervention* dramatically portrayed interventions in the United States and helped popularize the technique. However, there is no scientific evidence that interventions work. There is no need to try to shame a family member into getting treatment or confront them in a group setting without warning. Studies show that positive support is much more effective at helping someone change than humiliation or shame.

Rock Bottom

Another myth is that people need to "hit rock bottom" before they will change. In this myth, people with a substance-use disorder need to experience some truly terrible event to want to change. Examples may include homelessness or the threat of death due to medical conditions. This idea is completely false.

Most people with an SUD get better before experiencing any terrible events due to their condition. However, the myth of rock bottom can have terrible consequences. Sometimes, family members or friends who believe in it will refuse to help people with SUDs in the mistaken belief they are helping them hit rock bottom. In reality, difficult situations like homelessness and untreated health issues are not part of recovery. They increase a person's risk of bad outcomes from an SUD and should never be encouraged.

Medication Is Just Another Drug

A third myth revolves around medication that is used to treat OUD, especially methadone. There is a mistaken belief that methadone is the same as heroin or prescription opioids. While methadone is an opioid, it is also an effective treatment tool for OUD. Most people on methadone do not misuse it in the way that they misuse other opioids. This makes it very helpful for people trying to quit using opioids.

Methadone allows people to break the habit of always thinking about their next dose of opioids. They can start getting their life on track and building productive habits. Methadone also comes with many benefits over other recovery methods, such as a much lower risk of death by overdose. Therefore, it is a very dangerous myth that someone on methadone is not actually sober or getting their life together. Pressure to quit methadone early can result in a relapse.

MEDICATION-ASSISTED TREATMENT

One of the most successful treatment options for OUD is medication-assisted treatment (MAT). In the United States, MAT uses one of three medications to help prevent relapse and overdose: methadone, naltrexone, or buprenorphine. The Food and Drug Administration (FDA) has approved these three only, although there are trials for other drugs to be used in the future.

Each of these three medications has different benefits and is used in different ways. During MAT, a person also receives counseling and the opportunity to get their life back on track without misusing opioids. MAT is rarely the first treatment option for OUD. However, if a person has a long history of opioid misuse and relapse, it is one of the most effective.

MAT works by normalizing brain chemistry. After long-term opioid misuse, the brain is accustomed to being flooded by opioids. When a person quits, their brain chemistry is thrown off. This results in withdrawal symptoms, intense cravings, and a high chance of relapse. MAT makes this process easier.

The benefits of MAT are unchallenged in the medical and scientific communities. MAT decreases the chance of relapse by preventing cravings. MAT also reduces the risk of overdose. After a person leaves a no-medication inpatient rehab, their risk of relapse and overdose is significant. MAT lowers this risk.

Despite these benefits, doctors and government-funded programs have been slow to adopt MAT. This is due to the stigma that MAT is simply giving drugs to people who are addicted to drugs. Luckily, attitudes have changed in recent years. More and more rehab facilities are offering MAT. However, the use of MAT is still quite low in young adults. It is typically unavailable to people under the age of sixteen, and people between the ages of sixteen and eighteen are rarely offered MAT. There is a push in medical circles to overcome this issue. In 2016, the American Academy of Pediatrics recommended that pediatricians—doctors who treat younger patients—consider MAT when treating adolescents with OUD.

Methadone

Methadone is the oldest FDA-approved drug for medication-assisted treatment of opioid dependence. Methadone is a long-lasting opioid agonist that is taken once a day. It works in a similar fashion to heroin or OxyContin by binding to opioid receptors

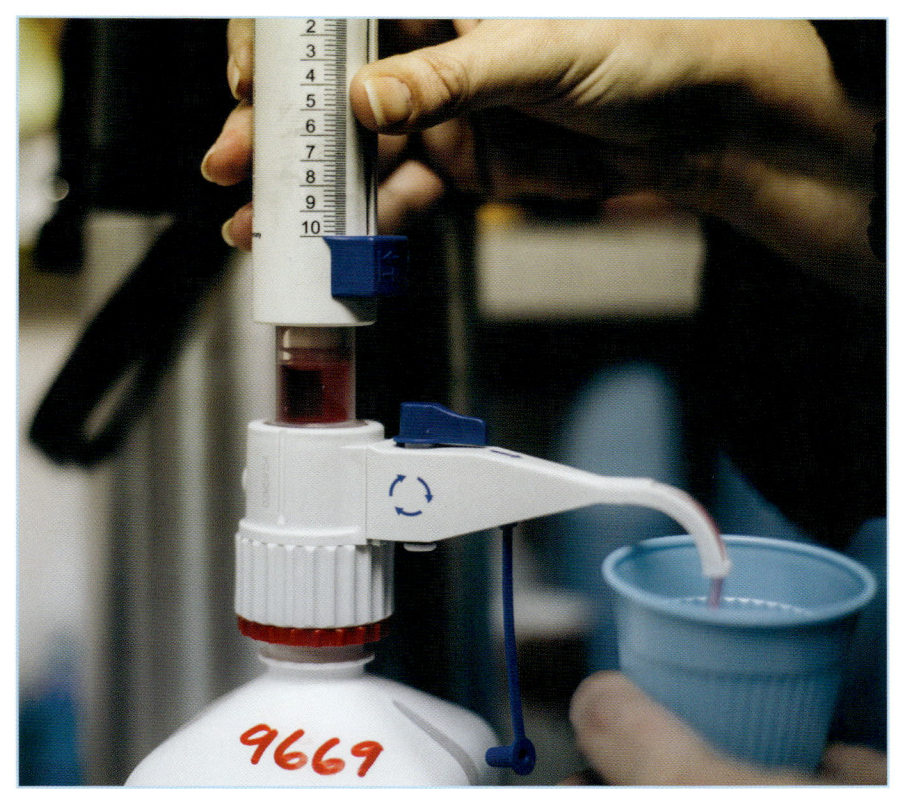

A health-care worker measures out methadone syrup.

in the brain, but people on methadone are given a small dose that does not result in a high. The fact that methadone binds to these receptors blocks other opioid agonists like heroin from doing so. This means that people on methadone who try to get high on opioids are typically unable to do so, preventing relapse. Methadone also reduces cravings.

When taken as directed, methadone is safe and effective. However, because it is an opioid agonist, there are some downsides to methadone. It can be used recreationally when not taken as directed. As a result, patients typically must go to a clinic or doctor's office each day to take methadone. Sometimes, they may eventually be allowed to take a prescription home, but at the beginning, going in every day is a major inconvenience.

The fact that methadone is an opioid agonist also means mixing it with other substances can be extremely dangerous. Adults on methadone maintenance are not supposed to drink alcohol. Some common anti-anxiety drugs are also rarely prescribed to people on methadone due to worries about combining the two drugs.

Methadone treatment typically lasts at least twelve months. Then, the patient and treatment provider may consider stopping methadone or continuing it longer. It is possible for people under the age of eighteen to be prescribed methadone for

MAT. Usually, they are required to show that they have relapsed multiple times after other treatment options. It also requires parental permission.

Naltrexone

Naltrexone is an opioid antagonist, like Narcan. This means it bind to opioid receptors in the brain, but it does not cause the effects associated with opioids like euphoria and pain relief. Instead, it blocks opioid agonists like heroin and OxyContin from working.

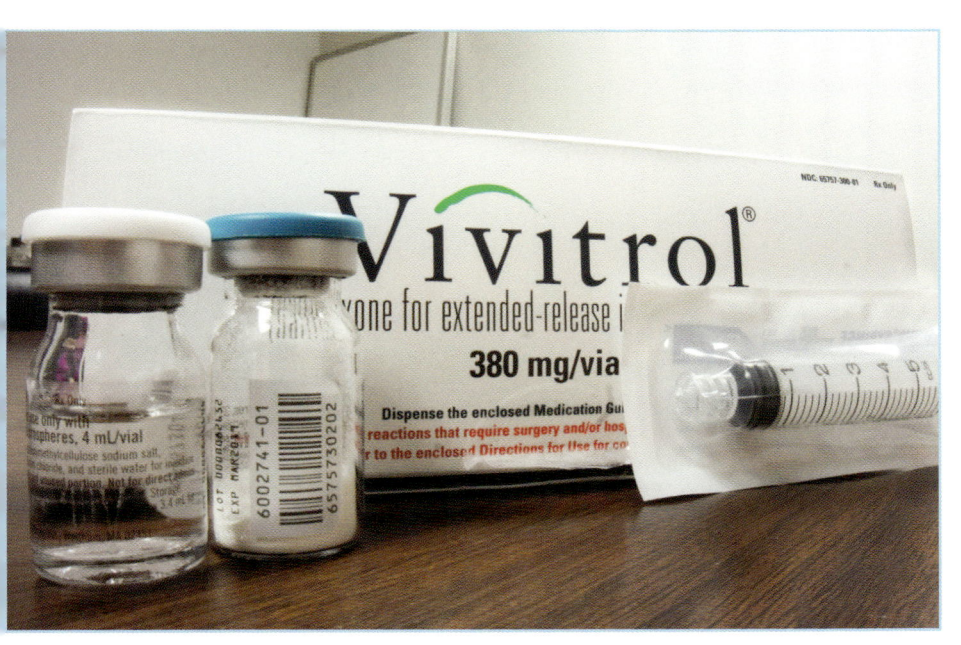

Vivitrol is a brand-name formulation of naltrexone.

Turning Tragedy into Change

As the opioid epidemic has spread across North America, the number of fatal overdoses has risen. In 2017, about seventy-two thousand people died from drug overdoses in the United States. More than two-thirds of these deaths involved an opioid. Many more people die due to health problems or suicide related to opioid misuse. Behind these numbers are stories of loss and grief. The tragedy of losing a loved one to opioid misuse has affected communities and families across the United States.

Many family members of people who lost their lives to opioids have transformed their grief into something positive. They have started organizations and charities to prevent further loss of life from opioids. One example is Gary Mendell's nonprofit organization, Shatterproof.

In 2011, Mendell lost his son Brian. Brian had fought against his opioid addiction for years before taking his own life. Brian had earlier spoken to his father about the stigma of opioid misuse: "Someday, people will realize that I am not a bad person. That I have a disease and I am trying my hardest."

The tragedy of Brian's loss inspired Mendell to start Shatterproof. Shatterproof works to end "the devastation addiction causes families." It promotes medically sound treatment for opioid addiction and works to change laws so that more people can get treatment.

Shatterproof and other organizations like it are at the forefront of change. They are helping to end the stigma around opioid misuse and help people recover. Often, it is the friends and family members of people who misuse opioids who spearhead these efforts.

As a result, someone must be completely sober before going on naltrexone. If they are not, naltrexone precipitates withdrawal, meaning withdrawal symptoms begin immediately upon taking naltrexone and are much more severe than usual. For this reason, a person must be off opioids for about a week before starting naltrexone. This is one downside of naltrexone, since detoxing off opioids can be quite difficult.

Once someone begins taking naltrexone, it reduces their cravings for opioids. If they take opioids, it also blocks their effects and therefore prevents relapse. One benefit of naltrexone is that it has no potential for misuse. Doctors frequently prescribe a month's supply, so there is no need to go to a clinic or doctor's office each day like with methadone.

Additionally, it is possible to get a monthly injection of naltrexone. This means people who use naltrexone do not even have to remember to take it each day.

Buprenorphine

Buprenorphine is a relatively new medication for the treatment of opioid dependency. The FDA approved it in 2002. Buprenorphine is a partial opioid agonist. It binds to opioid receptors in the brain, but not as strongly as methadone or heroin. This makes it well suited for use in MAT.

Because buprenorphine is a partial agonist, it has a "ceiling effect." Taking more than a moderate amount does not cause more euphoria or respiratory

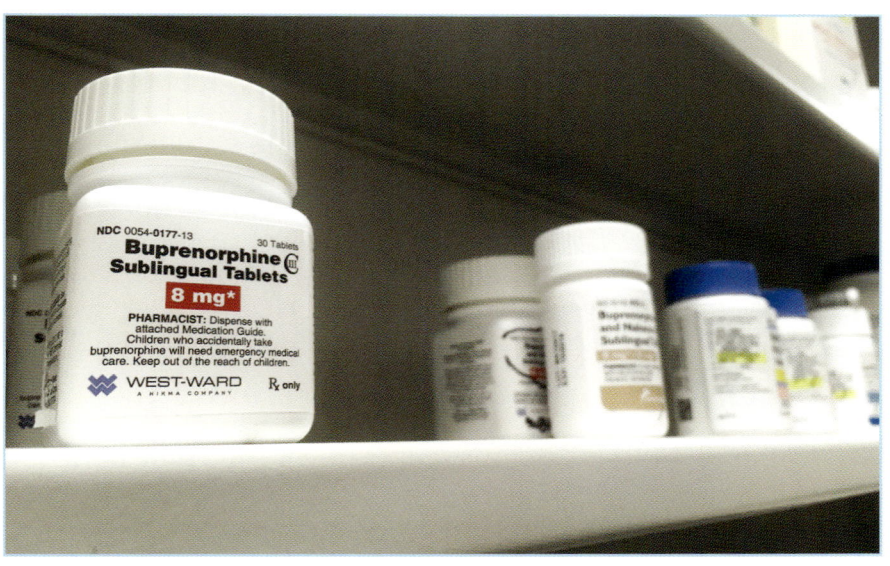

Buprenorphine is taken once a day, usually at home.

depression. This makes misuse and overdose unlikely. For someone with a history of opioid misuse, euphoria from buprenorphine is usually impossible. For someone with little history who misuses buprenorphine, euphoria and overdose are more likely. To prevent this, buprenorphine is often mixed with an opioid antagonist (the same one that is in Narcan). The combination of the opioid antagonist with the buprenorphine prevents misuse. The brand name of this formulation is Suboxone.

Like methadone, buprenorphine is taken just once a day. Due to its limited potential for misuse compared to methadone, buprenorphine is commonly prescribed rather than dispensed at a clinic or doctor's office. This means someone on buprenorphine can receive a supply of the drug and not have to arrange their routine around daily visits to receive it.

A person who begins buprenorphine treatment must go into withdrawal first. If they are not in withdrawal, the buprenorphine can precipitate withdrawal. However, unlike naltrexone, a person does not need to be completely off opioids to begin buprenorphine. The middle stages of withdrawal symptoms are typically enough.

Buprenorphine reduces cravings to use opioids and prevents withdrawal symptoms. It allows someone to focus on recovery and getting their life back together without worrying about getting opioids or completely detoxing. Furthermore, buprenorphine blocks the effects of opioid agonists like heroin or OxyContin because the buprenorphine binds to the opioid receptors in the brain. This leaves no free receptors for other opioids to bind to. As a result, buprenorphine prevents relapse by blocking the euphoria of other opioids if someone slips up and takes them.

THE ROAD TO RECOVERY

If you or someone you know misuses opioids, there is help available. The journey to fully recover from an addiction can seem long, but the first step is simple. Talk to a trusted adult or friend about the problem. Then, set up an appointment with a doctor or addiction specialist. They will be able to guide you through the process.

From counseling to MAT, there are many different options to help a person with an opioid use disorder. The symptoms of withdrawal can be managed. Support and medication can lessen cravings and help someone stay sober.

Just because someone has relapsed in the past does not mean they should not keep trying to quit misusing opioids. Most people relapse multiple times before succeeding. Keep trying. Reach out. Change your life or the life of someone you love for the better.

Glossary

adulterant Additives that make a substance less pure. When it comes to illegal drugs, adulterants may be dangerous.

analgesic A substance that lessens pain.

buprenorphine A drug that is used for medication-assisted treatment of opioid misuse.

cut To add adulterants to a drug to make it less pure.

dependence The state of needing to take a drug to avoid withdrawal.

detox To completely stop taking a drug and go through withdrawal.

Diagnostic and Statistical Manual of Mental Disorders, 5th Edition (DSM-5) The manual that mental health professionals use to diagnose mental illness.

Food and Drug Administration (FDA) The agency in the United States that approves prescription drugs for use.

medication-assisted treatment (MAT) This treatment uses prescription medication to help people with opioid use disorder.

methadone An opioid that is used in medication-assisted treatment.

microscopic An amount so small it cannot be seen with the naked eye.

naltrexone A drug that is used in medication-assisted treatment for opioid misuse. It can be injected once a month or taken by pill daily.

Narcan A preparation of a drug that reverses an opioid overdose when applied.

opioid A drug that binds to the opioid receptors in the brain. Opioids include illegal drugs like heroin and many prescription painkillers like Vicodin and OxyContin.

opioid agonist Opioid agonists are drugs that activate the opioid receptors in the brain. They lessen pain but also cause a high in large doses, which can lead to misuse. Opioid agonists include heroin and prescription medications.

opioid antagonist Opioid antagonists bind to opioid receptors in the brain but do not activate the receptors in the way that opioids do. Antagonists do not lessen pain or cause someone to get high. Antagonists reverse opioid overdoses and block the effects of opioids like heroin.

opioid use disorder (OUD) A diagnosable condition that involves a problematic pattern of opioid misuse.

oxycodone A prescription opioid that is commonly misused.

OxyContin A well-known brand name of extended release oxycodone.

relapse To begin using drugs again after trying to stop.

respiratory depression Slow or shallow breathing; during an opioid overdose, respiratory depression can lead someone to stop breathing and die unless they receive medical aid.

sober Not under the influence of or addicted to drugs or alcohol.

stigma Something that is disapproved of by society.

substance use disorder (SUD) A problematic pattern of misusing a drug or alcohol.

Vicodin A well-known brand name of hydrocodone (an opioid) and acetaminophen (Tylenol) that is commonly prescribed in the United States.

withdrawal The process or symptoms of quitting a drug that a person is dependent on.

Further Information

BOOKS

Greek, Joe. *Coping with Opioid Abuse*. Coping. New York: Rosen Publishing Group, 2017.

Hyde, Natalie. *Opioid Crisis*. Get Informed— Stay Informed. New York: Crabtree Publishing, 2018.

Johanson, Paula. *Critical Perspectives on the Opioid Epidemic*. Analyzing the Issues. Berkeley Heights, NJ: Enslow Publishing, 2017.

WEBSITES

How Opioid Addiction Occurs

https://www.mayoclinic.org/diseases-conditions/prescription-drug-abuse/in-depth/how-opioid-addiction-occurs/art-20360372

The Mayo Clinic outlines what an opioid addiction is and provides two short videos about the ongoing opioid epidemic.

The Overdose Antidote: How Narcan Works

https://whyy.org/segments/the-overdose-antidote-how-narcan-works/

Learn how Narcan reverses an opioid overdose and how it is administered.

What to Do If You Have a Problem with Drugs: For Teens and Young Adults
https://www.drugabuse.gov/related-topics/treatment/what-to-do-if-you-have-problem-drugs-teens-young-adults
Take an in-depth look at what do if you have a drug problem on this site hosted by the National Institute of Drug Abuse.

VIDEOS

How the Powerful Opioid Fentanyl Kills
https://www.cbc.ca/news/canada/manitoba/how-the-powerful-opioid-fentanyl-kills-1.3864676
CBC News explains how a fentanyl overdose results in death.

Why the Human Brain Loves Opioids
https://youtu.be/fVdXlB89QOA
PBS NewsHour looks at how opioids work on receptors in the brain, and how this leads to addiction.

Bibliography

Boston University Medical Center. "Medications Underutilized When Treating Young People with Opioid Use Disorder." *ScienceDaily*, June 19, 2017. https://www.sciencedaily.com/releases/2017/06/170619125851.htm.

Cicero, Theodore J., Matthew S. Ellis, Hilary L. Surat, and Stephen P. Kurtz. "The Changing Face of Heroin Use in the United States: A Retrospective Analysis of the Past 50 Years." *JAMA Psychiatry* 71, no. 7 (July 2014): 821–826.

Cragg, Amber, et al. "Risk Factors for Addiction among Patients Receiving Prescribed Opioids: A Systematic Review Protocol." *Systematic Reviews* 6, no. 1 (December 28, 2017). doi:10.1186/s13643-017-0642-0.

Des Jarlais, Don C. "Harm Reduction in the USA: The Research Perspective and an Archive to David Purchase." *Harm Reduction Journal* 14, no. 1 (July 26, 2017). https://doi.org/10.1186/s12954-017-0178-6.

Haydon, Ian. "How Opioids Reshape Your Brain, and What Scientists Are Learning about Addiction." *Philadelphia Inquirer*, August 1, 2018. https://medicalxpress.com/news/2018-08-opioids-reshape-brain-scientists-addiction.html.

Laucius, Joanne. "In the Trenches of Ottawa's Opioid Epidemic: 'A Good Kid with a Big Heart' Dies of Suspected Overdose." *Ottawa Citizen*, April 19, 2018. https://ottawacitizen.com/news/local-news/in-the-trenches-of-ottawas-opioid-epidemic-a-good-kid-with-a-big-heart-dies-of-suspected-overdose.

NIDA. "The True, Deadly Scope of America's Fentanyl Problem." May 1, 2018. https://www.drugabuse.gov/about-nida/noras-blog/2018/05/true-deadly-scope-americas-fentanyl-problem.

SAMHSA. "Medication and Counseling Treatment." Last updated September 28, 2015. https://www.samhsa.gov/medication-assisted-treatment/treatment.

———. "Opioids." Last updated on February 23, 2016. https://www.samhsa.gov/atod/opioids.

Seaman, Andrew M. "More Than a Third of U.S. Adults Prescribed Opioids." *Scientific American*, August 1, 2017. https://www.scientificamerican.com/article/more-than-a-third-of-u-s-adults-prescribed-opioids.

White, William L., and William R. Miller. "The Use of Confrontation in Addiction Treatment: History, Science and Time for Change. *Counselor* 8, no. 4 (2007): 12–30.

Index

About the Author

Derek Miller is a writer and educator from Salisbury, Maryland. He is the author of numerous books for middle school and high school students, including *Helping Yourself, Helping Others: Dealing with Cyberbullying.* In his free time, Miller likes to read and travel with his wife.